Royally Suited:
Harry and Meghan
in their own words

Royally Suited:
Harry and Meghan
in their own words

Published by
Medina Publishing Ltd
310 Ewell Road
Surbiton
Surrey KT6 7AL
medinapublishing.com

©Phil Dampier 2018

2 4 6 8 9 7 5 3 1

ISBN 978-1-911487-28-9

Printed and bound by Interak Printing House, Poland

CIP Data: A catalogue record for this book is available from the British Library.

Royally Suited:
Harry and Meghan
in their own words

Phil Dampier

Medina Publishing

Phil Dampier has been writing about the royal family for 31 years.

Between 1986 and 1991 he covered the royal beat for *The Sun*, Britain's biggest-selling daily newspaper. As a freelance journalist for the last 26 years, he has travelled to more than 60 countries following members of the House of Windsor, and his articles have been published in dozens of newspapers and magazines worldwide.

He was present in September 2017 when Prince Harry and Meghan Markle made their first appearance together at a public event, the Invictus Games in Toronto, Canada, and he will be reporting on their wedding for radio and TV stations worldwide.

CONTENTS

By the same author:

Diana: I'm Going to be Me, Barzipan Publishing, 2017

with Ashley Walton:

Prince Philip: A Lifetime of Wit and Wisdom, Barzipan Publishing 2017

Prince Philip: Wise Words and Golden Gaffes, Barzipan Publishing 2012 (4th reprint 2017)

White House Wit, Wisdom and Wisecracks, Barzipan Publishing 2013

SOURCES AND ACKNOWLEDGEMENTS

I personally witnessed some of Harry and Meghan's comments. Others have come from newspaper and magazine reports, and I am also grateful for material from the following books and blogs:

William and Harry, Katie Nicholl (Preface 2010)

Prince Harry The Inside Story, Duncan Larcombe (HarperCollins 2017)

Prince Harry Brother, Soldier, Son, Penny Junor (Hodder and Stoughton 2014)

The Tig, Meghan's Lifestyle Blog

FOREWORD

On 27 November 2017, Prince Charles's office announced that his youngest son Prince Harry and American actress Meghan Markle were engaged. Overnight they became one of the most famous pairings on the planet and were googled more than any other couple.

Their wedding in St George's Chapel at Windsor Castle on 19 May 2018 will be watched by hundreds of millions of people all over the world, and interest will only grow as they begin royal duties and start a family.

In this book I have told their story in their own words. What better way to get an insight into their history, interests and aspirations?

Using their own quotes, comments and writings, we learn how Harry suffered, and ultimately coped with, the tragic early death of his mother, Princess Diana. How his decade in the Army made him a man, and how he finally left behind his playboy image to become a mature and thoughtful crusader for good causes.

We see how Meghan came from a mixed-race background in her native California, was active in social issues from a young age, and moved to Toronto to become a successful actress in the legal drama 'Suits' while also pursuing humanitarian goals.

We also hear her thoughts on fashion, food and health issues, as fans hang on her every word and gesture, looking for inspiration. Together they will breath fresh life into the ancient institution of monarchy just as it needs it most.

Their amazing journey together is just beginning, so sit back and savour their story so far, and enjoy *Royally Suited: Harry and Meghan in their own words*.

Phil Dampier

January 2018

HARRY BEFORE MEGHAN

HARRY BEFORE
MEGHAN

When William told Diana: *'When I grow up, I want to be a policeman and look after you, mummy.'*
Harry said: *'Oh no, you can't. You've got to be king!'*

As a child, he would tell friends: *'Don't worry, our policemen will protect us from any baddies!'*

To father Charles at Crathie Church, the day after Diana's death in 1997: *'Are you sure mummy's dead?'*

As letters of condolence piled up at Balmoral, Harry asked: *'Can I open some?'*

As he, William and Prince Charles looked at bouquets of flowers outside the gates of Balmoral, Harry grabbed his father's hand and said: *'Look at this one Papa, read this one.'*

In 1993, nine-year-old Harry locked himself in the toilet of a train going to Cardiff on an away day with mum Diana and brother William. Diana pulled him out and then looked on as he stuck his head out of the speeding train and shouted: *'Oh my God, there's a train coming!'*

In 1995, Diana took her boys on a dangerous 10-mile trip white-water rafting in Colorado. When the white-knuckle trip was over Harry screamed: *'Mum that was great! I really enjoyed it, can we do it again?'*

William to Harry: *'It's so unfair, you always have weekends off from school. Matron won't let you get away with it again.'*
Harry replied: *'She will when she finds out it's to have tea with granny!'*

As a mischievous teenager, Harry shot dead a moorhen, which his father loved, at the family home Highgrove. William and Harry were called into the office of Eton housemaster Dr Andrew Gailey, who had been asked to investigate, and he told them: *'Your father is very upset because someone shot the moorhen.'*
William said: *'Which moorhen is that Dr Gailey?'*
To which Harry replied: *'The one you told me not to shoot!'*
Harry then rang his father and told him: *'I'm so sorry Papa, it was me, I shouldn't have done it.'*

Harry looking back: *To be honest, dinner conversations were the worst bit about being a child and listening to the boring people around me.'*

'You've got to give something back – you can't just sit there.'

Aged 18, Harry said about his mother: *'She had more guts than anyone else.'*

'I want to carry on the things that she didn't quite finish.'

'I have always wanted to, but was too young.'

'She got close to people and went for the sort of charities and organisations that everybody else was scared to go near, such as landmines in the Third World, and AIDS.'

In 2002, French barman Franck Ortet alleged that Harry would visit the Rattlebone Inn in Wiltshire with friends, get drunk and call him a *'Fucking Frog,'* **once saying to him:** *'Fuck off you Froggie, get back to your stupid country!'*

In 2003, when Princess Diana's former butler Paul Burrell published his memoirs *A Royal Duty,* **William and Harry issued a statement saying:** *'We cannot believe that Paul, whom was entrusted with so much, could abuse his position in such a cold and overt betrayal.'*

'It is not only deeply painful for the two of us but also for everyone else affected and it would mortify our mother if she were alive today and, if we might say so, we feel we are more able to speak for our mother than Paul. We ask Paul to bring these revelations to an end.'

In 2004, Harry spent two months of his gap year in Lesotho, where he fell in love with the people and vowed to help them in their battle against HIV-AIDS.

'This is a country that needs help,' **he said.**

He later asked ITV News to film a documentary, and said in an interview: *'I love children but that's probably because I've got an incredibly immature side to me.*

'I love children back home, but up here there's hundreds of children everywhere.'

'There are eight-year-olds looking after cattle.'

'The nicest thing out here is that they don't know who I am – I'm just a normal guy to them, which is really, really nice.'

'I'm only 19, but there is a lot of me that wants to say, "Ok, let's keep my mother's legacy going."'

'I try and be as normal as I can, to try and have a normal life before it gets too hectic.'

'I believe I've got a lot of my mother in me.'

'I just think she'd want us to do this, me and my brother.'

'I think I've got more time on my hands to be able to help.'

'We have both got our lives set out for us, but I think he's got his life really set out.'

Talking about his mother in the same interview:
'Unfortunately it's been a long time now – not for me but for most people – a long time since she died.'

'But it's just a shame that after all the good she's done, even this far on, people aren't bringing out the good in her.'

'There're people who want to bring out the bad stuff because bad news sells.'

'I don't want to take over from her, because I never will. I don't think anyone can, but I want to try and carry on, to make her proud.'

'Much as I'd like to be normal, I'm not normal, and my father reminds me of that the whole time.'

'I think the British media try to focus on the fact that I am a playboy, I am a party prince, all that sort of stuff, which I'm not.'

'I'm a teenager who goes out and has fun, and no matter what time I come out of a club, they're going to write that it was four o'clock in the morning.'

Asked about the pressure of being in the spotlight he said:
'Time after time it upsets me, but nobody will understand that other than my brother and myself. He and I are very close, obviously because of our mother.'

'Ever since our mother died, everyone recognises us around streets, you know, it's a bit awkward, but as I get older I can use it like my mother did.'

'She was just a normal woman who married my father and became this Queen of Hearts simply because she used her position basically and used her position in a good way, and that's what I want to do.'

'William is the one person on this earth who I can actually

really, you know, we can talk about anything. We understand each other and we give each other support.'

When Harry decided he wanted to set up the Sentebale charity to help youngsters in Lesotho, he stood up to his father – who thought he was too young to start his own charity – and said: *'I'm going to do this come hell or high water and nothing's going to get in the way, even though everyone's trying to stop me for obvious reasons.'*

'Why shouldn't I set up a charity because I'm too young? It's not a good enough reason.'

'It's very easy to find a reason not to do something, it's much more difficult sometimes to take something head on and challenge it, address it and make it happen.'

Asked what impact seeing suffering in Lesotho had on him, he said: *'It really hits you hard and makes you wake up and think, Jesus, I'm really very, very lucky.'*

'It sort of changes your temper with other people who don't appreciate it.'

'If you make a mistake you must own up to it.'

After watching the film premiere of Quantum of Solace:
'I've made a terrible boob – I've just told Daniel Craig that Sean Connery was the best James Bond!'

When the Queen was given her first mobile phone she asked Harry to record a voicemail greeting.
'Hey, wassup? This is Liz,' **he recorded.**

'*Sorry, I'm away from the throne. For a hotline to Philip, press one, for Charles, press two, and for the corgis, press three!*' **The Queen was amused when told about the hoax by her private secretary Robin Janvrin, who had called the number and** '*Got the shock of his life.*'

When Prince Charles married Camilla Parker Bowles in 2005, William and Harry issued a statement saying: '*We are both very happy for our father and Camilla, and we wish them all the luck in the future.*'

During an interview to mark his 21st birthday in 2005, Harry said of Camilla: '*To be honest with you, she's always been very close to me and William … But no, she's not the wicked stepmother.*

'*I'll say that right now.*'

'*Everyone has to understand that it's very hard for her.*'

'*Look at the position she's coming into.*'

'*Don't always feel sorry for me and William, feel sorry for her.*'

'*She's a wonderful woman and she's made our father very, very happy, which is the most important thing.*'

'*William and I love her to bits.*'

In an interview to mark his 21st birthday, Harry talked about the media and his then-girlfriend, Chelsy Davy. '*There is truth and there is lies,*' **he said.**

'And unfortunately, I cannot get the truth across because I don't have a newspaper column – although I'm thinking of getting one!

'It does irritate me because obviously, I get to see how upset she gets, and I know the real her, but that's something we deal with on our own time and unfortunately, it's not something I can turn round to people, to the press, and say, "She's not like that, she's like this." That is my private life.'

'I would love to tell everyone how amazing she is, but once I start talking about that, I have left myself open.'

In 2005, Harry went to the Royal Military Academy at Sandhurst to be trained as an officer. 'I wouldn't have joined the Army unless I was going to fight,' **he said.**

'If they said I couldn't then there's no way I would drag my sorry arse through Sandhurst.'

'The last thing I would want to do is to have my soldiers sent away to Iraq or somewhere like that and for me to be held back at home twiddling my thumbs, thinking 'What about David or Derek or whoever?' It's not the way anyone should really work.'

Talking about the tough training he said: 'The first five weeks were a bit of a struggle.'

'Nobody's really supposed to love it, it's Sandhurst … you get treated like a piece of dirt to be honest.'

'I do enjoy running down a ditch full of mud, firing bullets; it's the way I am.'

'I love it.'

'When I have left, I'll have to make a special effort to visit William, for comedy value, just so he can salute me.'

'Every year we get closer.'

'It's amazing how close we've become.'

'We have even resorted to hugging each other.'

After training at Sandhurst Harry celebrated with a drunken night out at lap-dancing club Spearmint Rhino. He asked dancer Mariella Butkute: *'Why don't you try to get a better job?'*

When she asked him if he wanted a 'personal' dance he replied: *'I've got a really beautiful girlfriend, I wouldn't want to have a dance because that would be like cheating on her.'*

In an interview before a Wembley concert in July 2007, to mark the tenth anniversary of Diana's death, Harry said: *'She was a happy, fun bubbly person who cared for so many people.'*

'She's very much missed by not only us, but by a lot of people and I think that's all that needs to be said, really.'

Talking about the accident which killed Diana he said: *'For me personally, whatever happened that night ... in that tunnel ... no one will ever know.'*

'I'm sure people will always think about that the whole time.'

'It's weird because I think that when she passed away, there was never that time, there was never that sort of lull.'

'There was never that sort of peace and quiet for any of us.'

'Her face was always splattered on the paper [sic] the whole time.'

'Over the last ten years, I personally feel as though she has been … she's always there.'

'She's always been a constant reminder to both of us and everyone else.'

'When you're being reminded about it, it does take a lot longer and it's a lot slower.'

'We know we have certain responsibilities, but within our private life and within certain other parts of our life we want to be as normal as possible.'

'Yes, it's hard because to a certain respect we will never be normal.'

At the concert on July 1 2007, Harry went on stage with William and shouted: 'Hello Wembley!'

'This evening is about all that our mother loved in life. Her music, her dance, her charities and her family and friends.'

At the memorial service on August 31 in the Guards Chapel, St James's, Harry told the congregation: 'William and I can separate life into two parts.'

'There were those years when we were blessed with the physical presence beside us of both our mother and father.'

'And then there are the ten years since our mother's death. When she was alive we completely took her for granted, her unrivalled love of life, laughter, fun and folly.'

'She was our guardian, friend and protector.'

'She never once allowed her unfaltering love for us to go unspoken or undemonstrated.'

'She will always be remembered for her amazing public work.'

'But behind the media glare, to us, just two loving children, she was quite simply the best mother in the world.'

'We would say that, wouldn't we? But we miss her.'

'She kissed us last thing at night. Her beaming smile greeted us from school.'

'She laughed hysterically and uncontrollably when sharing something silly she might have said or done that day.'

'She encouraged us when we were nervous or unsure.'

'She – like our father – was determined to provide us with a stable and secure childhood.'

'To lose a parent so suddenly at such a young age – as others have experience – it is indescribably shocking and sad.'

'It was an event which changed our lives forever, as it must have done for everyone who lost someone that night.'

'But what is far more important to us now, and into the future, is that we remember our mother as she would have wished to be remembered, as she was – fun-loving, generous, down-to-earth, entirely genuine.'

'We both think of her every day. We speak about her and laugh together at all the memories.'

'Put simply, she made us, and so many other people, happy. May this be the way that she is remembered.'

In 2008, Harry was posted to Afghanistan with his regiment the Blues and Royals, part of the Household Cavalry. A previous posting to Iraq had been abandoned because of security concerns.

'I feel a huge sense of relief, a bit of excitement, a bit of phew, finally get the chance to actually do the soldiering that I wanted to do ever since I joined.'

Asked if he sometimes wished he wasn't a prince, he replied: *'I wish that quite a lot actually.'*

'I just want to put it into practice and do the job ... and essentially help everybody else ... and do my bit.'

Asked about his job as a battlefield air controller calling in air strikes, patrolling in Helmand Province and firing on militants: *'You do what you have to do, what's necessary to save your own guys.'*

'If you need to drop a bomb, worst case scenario, then you will, but then that's just the way it is.'

'It's not nice to drop bombs, but to save lives that's what happens.'

'Terry Taliban and his mates, as soon as they hear air, they go to ground, which makes life a little bit tricky.'

Harry chatted to pilots who did not know who he was, talking about their homes and families when it was quiet: 'It's good to be relaxed and have a good chat.'

'When you know things are hairy, then you need to obviously turn your game face on and do the job.'

When Harry chatted at length to one female pilot, his commanding officer told him: 'Flirt with her any longer and you'll have to get a room.'
Harry replied: 'Does that count as the Mile-High Club?'

Harry spent Christmas Day in the burnt-out town of Garmsir with the Ghurkas, remarking: 'Not your typical Christmas.' **Adding:** 'But Christmas is over-rated anyway.'

On patrols in an armoured vehicle: 'I can't wait to get back and just sit on a sofa.'

'It's going to be ridiculous after bouncing around in a turret. My hips are bruised, my arse is bruised.'

'Just walking around with some of the locals or the Afghan National Police – they haven't got a clue who I am – it's fantastic.'

'What am I missing the most? Nothing really.'

'Music – we've got music, we've got light, we've got food. No, I don't miss the booze.'

'It's nice just to be here with all the guys and just mucking in as one of the lads … it's bizarre.'

'I haven't really had a shower for four days, haven't washed my clothes for a week, and everything seems completely normal.'

'I think this is about as normal as I'm ever going to get.'

'Hopefully my mother would be proud. She would be looking down having a giggle about the stupid things that I've been doing, like going left when I should have gone right … William sent me a letter saying how proud he reckons that she would be.'

Using the pseudonym Spike Wells, Harry commented on Facebook with his then-girlfriend Chelsy Davy, telling her: 'Fucking cold here – like insanely cold, bit weird! Anyhoo, gotta go, lots of love to you, probably see you soon unfortunately for you, hee hee! Laters, ginge!'

After returning from Afghanistan: 'I wouldn't say I'm a hero at all. I'm no more of a hero than anyone else.'

'If you think about it there's thousands and thousands of troops out there.'

'I don't want to sit around Windsor because I generally don't like England that much and it's nice to be away from all the press and the papers and all the general shit they write.'

When the British inquest into the death of Princess Diana ended in April 2008 after six months, the jury returned a majority verdict that Diana and Dodi Fayed had been unlawfully killed by the 'grossly negligent driving of the following vehicles and the Mercedes' in which they died. They added that additional factors were the alcohol intake of the driver Henri Paul, who also died, and the fact the couple were not wearing seat-belts.

William and Harry issued a statement saying: *'We agree with their verdicts and are both hugely grateful for the forbearance they have shown in accepting such significant disruption to their lives over the past six months.'*

They added: *'Finally the two of us would like to express our most profound gratitude to all those who fought so desperately to save our mother's life on that tragic night.'*

Talking about the 2008 wedding of his cousin Peter Phillips to Canadian Autumn Kelly: *'Someone had the bright idea to have a mirrored dance floor at the reception, can you imagine how crazy that was?'*

Asked if he was worried people could see up the skirt of his girlfriend, he replied: *'Never mind Chelsy, it was my grandmother* [The Queen] *I was worried about!'*

In 2009, Harry and William went on a training course at RAF Shawbury to learn to fly helicopters. *'It's hard work but I'm better than William, which is all that matters,'* said Harry, in a BBC interview.

'I've always had a love of helicopters. I've always wanted to be a

pilot, mainly of helicopters rather than fixed wing, even though I'm under the impression that fixed wings are slightly easier to fly than helicopters.'

For six months, the brothers shared a cottage near the base: *'The first time and the LAST time, I can assure you of that,'* **said Harry.**

When William revealed his brother snores a lot, Harry said: *'Oh, God, they'll think we share a bed now!'*

'We're brothers, not lovers!'

After England's disastrous 0-0 draw with Algeria in the 2010 World Cup in South Africa, William and Harry went into the dressing room, and William tried to cheer up the players by using military analogies and telling them they were strong. Afterwards Harry told him: *'Oh, they'll have really enjoyed that – being told how to play better by a posh soldier!'*

At a fundraiser in Barbados in 2010, Harry met singer and TV host Cilla Black and said: *'I didn't expect you to be here!'* **To which she replied:** *'Surprise, Surprise.'* **Harry said:** *'I knew you would say that.'*

When William and Kate announced their engagement in November 2010, Harry said: *'I'm enormously pleased that William finally popped the question.'*

'I've known Kate for years and it's great that she is now becoming part of the family.'

'I always wished for a sister, and now I have one.'

In a 2011 US TV interview, he said: *'It was a big decision for William bring Kate into the family.'*

'He has done the right thing – waited and done what he feels is right.'

'Are you ready?' **said to his brother as they were about to leave St James's Palace before Prince William's 2011 wedding in Westminster Abbey.**

In 2012, Harry represented the Queen on a tour to Belize, Jamaica, the Bahamas, and Brazil. In Belize, he said: *'The Queen remembers so fondly her visits to this beautiful realm and speaks of the warmth of welcome she received on her most recent visit in 1994.'*

'I'm only sorry she can't make it and you're stuck with me!'

In Jamaica, he told a state banquet: *'I count it a great privilege to be standing here tonight, representing the Queen in Jamaica on her Diamond Jubilee.'*

'Her Majesty has asked me to extend her great good wishes to you all, and is sorry that she can't be here...but don't worry, cos every liddle ting gonna be aright!'

At a party to mark Jamaica's 50 years of independence, he was given a £300 bottle of Appleton Estate rum by islander Joyce Spence, who was surprised when he asked: *'Have you got another one for my big brother?'*

'The Queen is an inspiration and she combines all her virtues as a leader and as a Head of State, with those of

being a wonderful, caring grandmother – to whom we, her grandchildren, are utterly devoted.'

'As for me, I haven't been here for long, but – wow – if I had, I'm not sure my grandmother would get me back.'

He then moved onto Brazil where he was greeted by screaming fans at the top of Sugar Loaf Mountain, and said: *'Everything about Rio makes you want to dance.'*

'I'm just so thankful that my brother isn't here because he might actually do it – and that would not be cool!'

'I've heard so much about Rio over the years, in fact ever since my father told me about a certain dance he once had with a beautiful girl called Pinah.'

'It just seems to have stuck in his mind for some reason.'

After a video to promote British culture was shown, Harry said: *'That was David Beckham – apparently he used to play football.'*

After playing rugby on the beach with youngsters: *'One plea to all Brazilians though. Please, please, if we show you how to play rugby, don't do what you've done with football and leave us wishing we hadn't!'*

In Sao Paolo, he said: *'The most important thing for me in life is kids.'*

'I don't know whether I got that from my mum and my father. I just have this massive kid inside me.'

'I've always had that connection with kids and I always will hopefully.'

Talking to reporters at the end of the trip he said: 'I tell you what, it's been an emotional trip.'

'I'm absolutely exhausted, but the warmth of the reception that we've received from every single country that we've been to – including Brazil – has been utterly amazing.'

'I personally had no idea how much influence the Queen has on all these countries.'

'And to me that's been very humbling and I was actually quite choked up at times seeing the way that they've celebrated her 60 years.'

'She's thousands of miles away to some of these countries and yet they celebrate her in the way they did, and made me feel as one of them, so I couldn't thank them more.'

He spoke to the Queen before he left, saying: 'We had a great chat. She wished me luck and she said, "Enjoy it, I hope you do me proud." It was a typical grandmother-to-grandson chat.'

'I just hope that my grandmother is proud of what we've done.'

Talking about the Queen at the end of the tour he said: 'She's funny. I think she gets it from my grandfather.

'They are very funny together.'

'My family is the same as any other when it comes to humour

behind closed doors – though I'd like to think I was funnier than my grandmother!'

In May 2012, Harry received a humanitarian award in Washington from the Atlantic Council for his work with military veterans.

In a moving speech, he said: *'It would be wrong of me to speak for these heroes, but not presumptuous of me to pay tribute to them; so many of our servicemen and women have made the ultimate sacrifice; so many lives have been lost and so many changed forever by the wounds that they have suffered in the course of their duties.'*

'They have paid a terrible price to keep us safe and free.'

'The very least we owe them is to make sure that they and their brave families have everything they need through the darkest days – and in time, regain the hope and confidence to flourish again.'

'For these selfless people, it is after the guns have fallen silent, the din of battle quietened, that the real fight begins – fight that may last the rest of their lives.'

'Watching a fellow comrade injured or killed – these are experiences that remain with you for life, both physically and mentally.'

On the Queen's 'parachute jump' into the 2012 Olympic stadium in London: *'She was an unbelievably good sport – I can't quite believe it when I see those pictures back.'*

On cousin Zara winning an Olympic equestrian silver medal: *'We, as cousins, are very, very proud.'*

'It now explains why we never get to see her because she is always riding.'

'The support from the British public is something else.

'We've had the chance to be at quite a few of the events, and just to feel the buzz of the British public getting behind the teams is astonishing.'

Harry said his money was on Usain Bolt to win his races: *'Because, obviously, I'm not allowed to compete.'*

Talking about Bolt's influence he said: *'There's kids back in Jamaica now who started running or doing track events simply because they look up to him…he's a wonderful example for his country, for the nation, for the world.'*

Harry was the senior royal at the closing ceremony saying in a message: *'The games will stay in the hearts and minds of people all over the world for a very long time to come.'*

'I congratulate all the athletes who have competed. They have shown us that there are few boundaries to human endeavour. The athletes have captured the imagination of the world and the spirit of the Olympics represents a magnificent force for positive change.'

Talking later about his ill-fated 'lost weekend' in Las Vegas in 2012, when he was photographed playing naked strip-billiards in a hotel room with a group of girls he had just met:

'I probably let myself down, I let my family down, I let other people down.'

'But at the end of the day I was in a private area and there should have been a certain amount of privacy that one should expect.'

'It was probably a classic example of me being too much Army, and not enough prince – it's a simple case of that.'

Talking about a possible future wife, Harry told CBS news: *'I'm not so much searching for someone to fulfil the role but obviously, you know, finding someone who would be willing to take it on.'*

On his second posting to Afghanistan, Harry was based at Camp Bastion as a helicopter pilot, and returned home in January 2013.

He said in an interview: *'I hate it, being stuck here, I'd much rather be out with the lads in a patrol base.'*

'It's a pain in the arse being stuck in Bastion.'

'Going into the cookhouse with hundreds of people – it's frustrating.'

I go into the cookhouse and everyone has a good old gawp, and that's one thing that I dislike about being here.'

'Essentially, we just sit inside the tent and play computer games, watch movies and play uckers [**a board game**] *while we wait for the phone to go.'*

'During my flying course, I should have probably done a lot more reading.'

'Every now and then a written test would come up and I'd be absolutely useless.'

'Every time you run to the aircraft you get that adrenalin rush, and when you get to the aircraft you've got to try and slow yourself down because if the adrenalin is pumping too much and you rush, you're going to miss something.'

'We are doing as much as we can to make sure that the guys on the ground aren't being shot at, and if they are being shot at we go to where they're being shot at and we do what we have to do.'

'There's a lot of pressures, obviously, when we go and support the Americans or when we're escorting the Tricky [**mobile hospital**] ... but essentially I think it's less stressful being up here than it is down there.'

'We don't have to put on all the kit and walk around through the desert, sweating our balls off.'

Asked if he had made a kill, he said: 'Lots of people have. 'Take a life to save a life. That's what we revolve around I suppose.'

'If there's people doing bad stuff to our guys, we'll take them out of the game.'

'It's not the reason I decided to do this job. I did it to get back out here and carry on with a job.'

'It's a joy for me because I'm one of those people who loves playing PlayStation and Xbox, so with my thumbs I like to think I'm probably quite useful.'

'I'd never want to be stuck behind a computer desk.

'Normal for me? I don't know what normal is any more, I never really have done.'

'There are three parts of me, one obviously wearing the uniform, one being Prince Harry, and the other one which is the private sort of me behind closed doors.'

'I don't believe there is any such thing as a private life any more.'

'I'm not going to sit here and whinge.

'Everybody knows about Twitter and the Internet and stuff like that.'

'Every single mobile phone has got a camera on it now.'

'You can't move an inch without someone judging you, and I suppose that's the way life goes.'

Revealing that his father told him not to read newspapers, he said: 'Of course I read it.'

'If there's a story and something's been written about me I want to know what's being said, but all it does is just upset me and anger me that people can get away with writing the stuff they do.'

'Not just about me but about everything and everybody.'

At a swanky cocktail party in Colorado in 2013, Harry was handed a glass of Pimm's by a waiter, and said: *'I didn't realise you had Pimm's in America!'*

At a military rehabilitation centre in Bethesda, Maryland, he told wounded warriors: *'We've got nothing like this back in the UK.'*

'You guys, as Americans, are used to the technology – we are always behind.'

When told Kate was expecting a baby: *'It's about time. I can't wait to be an uncle.'*

'I'm thrilled for both of them.'

After Prince George was born on July 22 2013, Harry was asked about his nephew: *'He's about this long and this wide.'*

'It's fantastic to have an addition to the family.'

'I only hope my brother knows how expensive my baby-sitting charges are!'

In March 2014, Harry took to the stage at the Wembley Arena in front of 12,000 young people for the first WE Day in the UK.

'For those of you who were expecting Harry Styles here, I apologise, and, no, I'm not going to sing!'

'*Our society faces some very significant challenges.*'

'*Each year approximately 100 million children are affected by disasters, such as the Syrian crisis. One million children there have had to flee the country.*'

'*Luckily, for most of us, it is unimaginable to picture leaving your home in the middle of the night, not knowing if you will ever return.*'

'*Some people don't think it's cool to help others; personally, I think it's the coolest thing in the world!*'

Inspired by the American Warrior Games for disabled servicemen and women, Harry created the Invictus Games, and the first event was held in London, in March 2014.

'*I have witnessed first-hand how the power of sport can positively impact the lives of wounded, injured and sick servicemen and women in their journey of recovery.*'

'*The Invictus Games will focus on what they can achieve post injury and celebrate their fighting spirit, through an inclusive sporting competition that recognises the sacrifice they have made.*'

In 2015, Harry left the army and issued a statement saying:
'*After a decade of service, moving on from the Army has been a really tough decision.*'

'*I consider myself incredibly lucky to have had the chance to do some very challenging jobs and have met many fantastic people in the process.*'

'From learning the hard way to stay onside with my colour Sergeant at Sandhurst, to the incredible people I served with during two tours in Afghanistan – the experiences I have had over the last ten years will stay with me for the rest of my life.'

'For that I will always be hugely grateful.'

'Inevitably, most good things come to an end and I am at a crossroads in my military career.'

'Luckily for me, I will continue to wear the uniform and mix with fellow servicemen and women for the rest of my life.'

'I am considering the options for the future and I am really excited about the possibilities ... so, while I am finishing one part of my life, I am getting straight into a new chapter. I am really looking forward to it.'

On conservation: 'I hate fox hunting. Not because it's not good to keep numbers down but because of the whole class thing.'

'Because people perceive it to be a bunch of toffs knocking back the Sloe gin and enjoying themselves masks the real issues.'

'I can talk for 20 minutes about wildlife conservation and make one comment about my love life and that gets all the headlines, very annoying.'

During a visit to New Zealand in May 2015, he gave an interview to Sky News and said: 'Inevitably what happens as you climb the ranks in the Army is that you will do more of a desk job.'

'A lot of guys that get to my age leave, and that is partly because a lot of guys join for the outside, for the excitement of running around in the bush with the soldiers.'

'William and I feel we need to have a wage, we need to work with normal people to keep ourselves sane and also to keep us ticking along.'

'I've got to a stage now in my life where I'm very happy.'

'I've done ten years in the services, there is part of me of course that would love to carry on doing that, but there needs to come a decision about responsibilities in this role, therefore I need to find something that will have an even balance.'

Asked about settling down and having children he said:
'There come times when you think now is the time to settle down, or now is not, whatever way it is, but I don't think you can force these things, it will happen when it's going to happen.'

'Of course, I would love to have kids right now, but there's a process that one has to go through and tours like this are great fun.'

'Hopefully I'm doing alright by myself. It would be great to have someone else next to me to share the pressure, but you know, the time will come and whatever happens, happens.'

On the New Zealand tour, a woman in the crowd told him:
'You look just like your father.'
He replied: *'I'm losing my hair like him, too!'*

'My father never really gets listened to, which is disappointing

because whatever he says normally is right about ten years ahead of when the problems actually happen.'

'I dread to think where I'd be without the army.'

'Bring back National Service – I've said that before.'

'You can make bad choices in life, but it's how you recover from those and which path you end up taking.'

On a visit to Soweto in South Africa in December 2015, Harry told youngsters to follow the good things he did, not the bad, adding: *'Don't do a "Vegas!"'*

Talking about the Army he said: *'It was the making of me. We call it the "University of Life".'*

On Nelson Mandela: *'He'll never be forgotten.'*

At the Ottery Youth Centre in Cape Town, he told youngsters who were rehabilitated gang members: *'My name is Prince Harry, the Queen of England's grandson, Princess Diana's son.'*

'I've come all the way from England to see you guys.'

'I'm interested to hear all your stories.'

'I didn't enjoy school at all.'

'I would like to have come to a place like this.'

'When I was at school I wanted to be the bad boy.'

'If you've got an older brother that's not into gangs, that's a huge positive.'

'Older brothers are supposedly the cool ones.'

'I'm a younger brother, but I'm much cooler than my older brother.'

On a visit to the Kruger National Park, Harry saw dead rhinos killed by poachers and said: *'Seeing huge carcasses of rhinos and elephants scattered across Africa, with their horns and tusks missing is a pointless waste of beauty.'*

Describing Kruger as a 'major killing field' he said: *'If current poaching rates continue, there will be no wild African elephants or rhinos left by the time children born this year, like my niece Charlotte, turn 25.'*

Opening a new centre for AIDS orphans in Lesotho: *'Although our situations couldn't have been more different, I felt an overwhelming connection to many of the children I met.'*

'We shared a similar feeling of loss, having a loved one, in my case a parent, snatched away so suddenly.'

'I, like them, knew there'd always be a gaping hole that could never be filled.'

At a birthday party for friend Anneke von Trotha in London in early 2016, Harry chatted to TV presenter Denise Van Outen, who revealed he told her: *'I'm not dating, and for the first time ever, I want to find a wife.'*

In an interview in May 2016, in Florida, he said: *'At the moment my focus is very much on work, but if someone slips into my life then that's absolutely fantastic.'*

'I am not putting work before the idea of family and marriage.'

'I just haven't had that many opportunities to get out there and meet people.'

'The other problem is that even if I talk to a girl that person is suddenly my wife and people go knocking on her door.'

'If, or when I do, find a girlfriend I will do my utmost to ensure we get to the point where we are actually comfortable with each other, before the massive invasion into her privacy.'

'Only somebody who was already in the public eye would be able to understand and handle everything that goes with being a Prince.'

MEGHAN BEFORE HARRY

MEGHAN BEFORE HARRY

'When I was about seven, I had been fawning over a boxed set of Barbie dolls. It was called the "Heart Family" and included a mom doll, a dad doll, and two children.'

'This perfect nuclear family was sold only in sets of white dolls or black dolls. I don't remember coveting one over the other, I just wanted one.'

'On Christmas morning, swathed in glitter-flecked wrapping paper, there I found my "Heart Family". A black mom doll, a white dad doll, and a child in each colour. My dad had taken the sets apart and customised my family.'

'Whatever I want I'm going to get.' **Said to a fellow teenager.**

Talking about completing a school census when she was 12:
'There I was, my curly hair, my freckled face, my pale skin, my mixed race, looking down at these boxes.'

'You could only choose one, but that would be to choose one parent over the other – and one half of myself over the other.'

'I put down my pen. Not as an act of defiance, but rather a symptom of my confusion.'

'When I went home that night, I told my dad what had happened. He said to me, "If that happens again, you draw your own box."'

'You create the identity you want for yourself, just as my ancestors did when they were given their freedom.'

'Because in 1865 – which is so shatteringly recent – when slavery was abolished in the United States, former slaves had to choose a name – a surname to be exact.'

'Perhaps the closest thing connecting me to my ever-complex family tree, my longing to know where I come from, and the commonality that links me to my bloodline, is the choice that my great-great-great-great-grandfather made to start anew.'

'He chose the last name "Wisdom". He drew his own box.'

'My mom has always called me "Flower" … since I was a little girl.'

'When I was 13 years old, my mom had me start getting facials in my hometown of Los Angeles.'

'It seemed so silly at the time, trekking in my school uniform to see a woman named Anika, who slathered my skin with Yon-Ka products and chatted away about the importance of eye cream.'

'My mum would give Anika a cheque (and usually some fruit she picked up for her at the farmer's market, because she's thoughtful that way) and we would drive home, with my mum, ever the little bird in my ear, saying, "You must always take care of your skin!"'

'I started doing mummy-and-me yoga with her when I was seven.'

'I was very resistant as a kid, but she said, "Flower, you will find your practice, just give it time."'

'I started working at a soup kitchen in Skid Row of Los Angeles when I was 13 years old, and the first day I felt really scared.'

'I was young, and it was rough and raw down there, and though I was with a great volunteer group, I just felt overwhelmed.'

'I remember one of my mentors (Mrs Maria Pollia) told me that "life is about putting others' needs above your own fears." That has always stayed with me.'

Speaking to a UN conference: *'Women need a seat at the table, they need an invitation to be seated there, and in some cases where this is not available, they need to create their own table.'*

'Being a feminist and being feminine aren't mutually exclusive.'

'I am proud to be a woman and a feminist.'

'A wife is equal to her husband, a sister to her brother – not better, not worse, they are equal.'

'UN Women has defined 2030 as the expiration date for gender inequality, and here's what's staggering: the studies show that at the current rate, the elimination of gender inequality won't be possible until 2095.'

'It isn't simply enough to talk about equality, we need to believe in equality, we need to work at it.'

'Kindness is the number one quality I look for in a man. You can see it in how he treats anyone – from a CEO to a housekeeper.'

'I was not a girl who grew up buying $100 candles. I was the girl who ran out of gas on her way to an audition.'

'It's really attractive if a man has a skill that you want to improve in yourself.'

'If you can learn from someone that's sexy.'

'My dad is Caucasian; my mom is African-American. I'm half black and half white.'

'Feeling too light in the black community, too mixed in the white community for castings.'

'I was labelled "ethnically ambiguous".'

'Was I Latina? Sephardic Jewish? Exotic Caucasian?'

Resisting scenes in 'Suits' where, as Rachel Zane, she was asked to strip off: 'The moment that Rachel starts to become a role model off camera and getting feedback or letters from young women or their moms going, "Oh my goodness, my daughter can look up to you and say I'm bi-racial, I can be like that too," that's when it becomes important.'

'I do a lot of work with UN Women, so I take it seriously.'

'Does the scene really need to open with Rachel in her skivvies?'

'No, I don't think that is necessary.'

'There is a lot of overlap when you're on TV and a lot of people often get separated from the idea of you being both beautiful and covered up, and I'm fortunate that I have bosses who respect me saying that.'

Refusing to appear in scenes where she enters wearing only a towel: 'I said no, I'm not doing it anymore, I'm not doing it. So, I rang the creator and I was like, "It's just gratuitous, we get it, we've already seen it once."'

'So, I think at a certain point you feel empowered enough to just say no.'

'I think it's a challenging thing to do if you don't know your own worth and your value for wanting to speak up.'

'When you're an auditioning actress years ago, so hungry for work, of course you're willing to do things like that.'

'For me, speaking up and being able to say I'm not going to do that anymore, has been a big shift for me personally.'

'I've never wanted to be a lady who lunches; I've always wanted to be a woman who works.'

'And this type of work is what feeds my soul and fuels my purpose.'

'If you deprive yourself of something, you're going to crave it more.'

'I definitely try to eat as clean as possible. Mostly fish and veggies, but I'm also a foodie, so on the weekend all bets are off.'

'Women are like tea bags. They don't realise how strong they are until they're in hot water.' **From Meghan's 1999 high school year book, paraphrasing Eleanor Roosevelt.**

'My 11-year-old self would be proud because while I may not have realised it at the time, I have always had a foot in the world of entertainment as well as the world of public service.'

'My life now is simply a more heightened version of the very reality in which I grew up.'

'And, truth be told, it's the most beautiful gift I never knew I always had.'

'When I get ready to go out, it's half an hour and we're out of the door. I want to have fun!'

'I was born and raised in Los Angeles, a California girl who lives

by the ethos that most things can be cured with either yoga, the beach, or a few avocados.'

In an article for *Time* magazine, Meghan wrote about the struggles with menstrual health issues faced by girls in developing countries: *'During my time in the field, many girls shared that they feel embarrassed to go to school during their periods.'*

'Ill-equipped with rags instead of pads, unable to participate in sports, and without bathrooms available to care for themselves, they often opt to drop out of school completely.'

In November 2013, Meghan met journalist Katie Hind in London, and asked her: *'Do you know this guy, Ashley Cole? He follows me and he keeps trying to talk to me on Twitter. He's trying really hard.'*

'He wants to go out on a date while I'm over here in London. What do you think? Do you know him?'

'I wasn't black enough for the black roles and I wasn't white enough for the white roles, leaving me somewhere in the middle as the ethnic chameleon who couldn't book a job.'

'I dream pretty big, but truly had no idea my life could be this awesome.'

May 2015, before she met Harry: 'I am the luckiest girl in the world without question.'

'When the air is filled with positive vibes, there is no winter cold that can block out the warmth of happy hearts.'

'I wear so much make-up for work that when I have a day off I don't like to wear it at all.'

'Throw kindness around like confetti.'

'You need to be your own Valentine. You need to cook that beautiful dinner, even when it's just you, wear your favourite outfit, buy yourself flowers and celebrate the self-love that gets muddled when we focus on what we don't have.'

'In my humble opinion, much of the art of decluttering your mind stems from decluttering your space – your sanctuary a la casa.'

On her 'food as medicine philosophy': *'It's easy to fall into the trap of rushing for a coffee when you hit that 4 p.m. slump.'*

'But I blend some apple, kale, spinach, lemon and ginger in my juicer in the morning and bring it to work.'

'I always find sipping on that is a much better boost than having a cup of espresso.'

'There is honestly nothing as delicious, or as impressive, in my opinion, as a perfectly roasted chicken. It's a game-changer. I bring that to dinner parties and make a lot of friends.'

On finding a dog: *'Adopt don't shop.'*

On flowers, particularly pink peonies: *'They make me so endlessly happy.'*

On her mother Doria Ragland: *'We can just have so much fun together and yet I'll still find so much solace in her support.'*

'That duality coexists the same way it would in a best friend. I'm always proud of this beautiful woman.'

'I was at home on a college break when my mom was called the N-word. We were leaving a concert and she wasn't pulling out of a parking space quickly enough.'

Meghan buys cleansing cloths in bulk, saying: *'They're great to keep in the car and on your nightstand. For when you have those horribly lazy nights that the thought of getting up to actually wash your face seems unbearable.'*

'Fragrance is my favourite thing. So much so that if I leave the house and I don't put any on, I'll turn around and go back home.'

'Drink a lot of water – it changes how you look. But I often forget to do it because I prefer wine!'

'Men really love to see hair down.'

'As I've gotten older, I like longer dresses, but my legs come up to my ears and I'm not very tall, so when I wear a short skirt I've got to be really conscious.'

'The culture, food, people and varied landscapes make Mexico a favoured destination of mine year after year.'

'Find your tribe ... love them hard.'

'Know when to give up and have a Margarita.'

'In a society that profits from your self-doubt, liking yourself is a rebellious act.'

New Year's resolutions: *'Run a marathon, stop biting my nails, stop swearing, re-learn French. These make my New Year's list nearly (actually every) single year.'*

'The swearing comes in lulls, triggered by being overworked or feeling mighty cheeky after a couple of drinks.'

'And when it comes to the biting of the nails – well, it still happens with a turbulent flight or a stressful day.'

'It's unladylike, but then again, so is the swearing. Dammit.'

'With fame comes opportunity, but it also includes responsibility – to advocate and share, to focus less on glass slippers and more on pushing through glass ceilings. And, if I'm lucky enough, to inspire.'

On Rachel Zane, her character in 'Suits': *'She's feisty, intelligent, classy and ambitious. And she's got a moral compass.'*

Her dream interviewee: *'It would have to be former US Secretary of State Madeleine Albright – she learned German on bed rest.'*

Meghan's thoughts on life: *'We are stars wrapped in skin – the light you are looking for has always been within.'*

'Shoot for the moon. Even if you don't hit it, you'll always land in the stars.'

Posting a photograph of her feet with the caption: *'No bad energy...sending good vibes...always in all ways.'*

On her self-doubt: *'My twenties were brutal – a constant battle with myself, judging my weight, my style, my desire to be as cool, as hip, as smart, as "whatever" as everyone else.'*

'My teens were even worse – grappling with how to fit in, and what that even meant."

'You need to know that you're enough. A mantra that has now engrained itself so deeply within me that not a day goes by without hearing it chime in my head.'

'That five pounds lost won't make you happier, that more make-up won't make you prettier, that the now-iconic saying from Jerry Maguire – "You complete me" – isn't true. You are complete with or without a partner. You are enough just as you are.'

'The best handwritten note I ever received was probably from my dad when I booked my very first pilot saying, "Meg, I knew this day would come, I'm so proud of you." I still have it in a little jewellery box by the side of my bed.'

At the end of June 2016, around the time she met Harry, Meghan met broadcaster Piers Morgan in a London pub after he had told her he was a big fan of 'Suits'.
"OMG, you're out of hospital and cheating on Mike with that sleaze-ball!' **he told her on social media, to which Meghan replied:** *'Hahahaha. Oh, this is when everyone starts to hate Rachel. Brutal. People wanted to kill me. Not Rachel ... ME. I never knew there were emojis of knives and guns. Thankfully, Rachel gets back on her pedestal.'*

'My dad's Caucasian, my mother's African-American, so I'm half white, half black. It caused me a lot of confusion when I

was young because it's not easy to be ethnically ambiguous in America. But I learned to embrace being a mixed-race woman.'

Talking about US gun crime she told Piers Morgan: *'I just wish more people in my country would make a stand about it. I've enjoyed living in Canada for the past five years, without Rambo and co.'*

'People say it's not the guns but mental illness, to which I say, so then why give mentally ill people legal access to buy guns? It's staggering. So many needless deaths.'

On critics: *'There's a great quote from the artist Georgia O'Keeffe, "I have already settled it for myself so flattery and criticism go down the same drain, and I am quite free." That really resonates with me.'*

Asked by Piers if she always wanted to be an actress she said: *'No! As a kid, I wanted to either be President of the United States or a news broadcaster like you.'*

'I'm also a trained calligrapher. I did all the cards and envelopes for Robin Thicke's wedding! We're losing the art of handwriting and it's such a shame.'

'There's still something incredibly romantic and special about a guy writing to a girl and putting pen to paper rather than emailing it, whether his writing is chicken scratch or looks like a doctor's note.'

Asked to name the most embarrassing thing she's ever done: *'Oh God, I was one of the briefcase girls on 'Deal Or No Deal.'* **[the US version]**

'I cringe myself when I think about it now, but it paid the rent. I was number 24, which nobody ever chose.'

'I'd stand there for hours in very cheap, very high heels waiting for someone to pick me so I could sit down again, and it hardly ever happened.'

'When I was 11, I saw this ad for dish soap powder that said, "Women all over America are fighting greasy pots and pans." I was so angry. I couldn't understand why it didn't say men as well.'

'My parents always told me if I believed something was wrong, I should try to fix it.

'So, I wrote to all sorts of people including Hillary Clinton, and the soap's manufacturers Procter and Gamble, demanding they change it. It worked – they altered the wording from 'women' to 'people."

She then read a text message and smiled, saying: 'I'm recently single again, so I've got a few guys being a little... persistent!'

'I'm just out of practice with the dating scene. I simply love my life, every ounce of it.'

'Because when you stop and look around, this life is pretty amazing.'

HARRY
AND MEGHAN

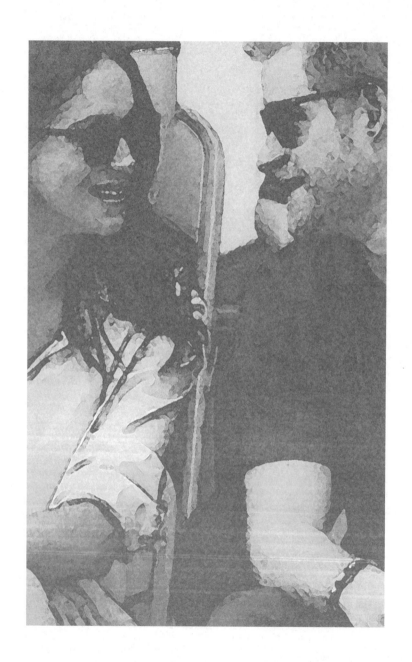

HARRY AND MEGHAN

On her 35th birthday in August 2016, Meghan said on The Tig (her lifestyle blog): '*I have to say that when I close my eyes and think of what I wish for, I come up with a blank. A big old happy blank.*'

'*I am feeling so incredibly joyful right now, so grateful and content that all I could wish for is more of the same.*'

Among Meghan's 'sustainable holiday celebration tips' on The Tig in December 2016: '*While there is no shortage of festivities demanding our attention at the moment, it's important that we never forget the well-being our god ol' Mama Earth.*'

'*Lower gas emissions by planning and avoiding multiple trips to the store.*'

'Two huge problems with not planning your meals is that you end up throwing away food, and you spend too much time taking grocery trips. Huddle and save.'

'Streamline your meals (even if they aren't exact) and make as few trips as possible. You're saving money, time and planet.'

When her character in 'Suits', Rachel Zane, got engaged, Meghan said: *'The fun part of Rachel getting engaged is that fans come up and say, "We're so happy for you, congratulations!" I'm like, "Well, Rachel's getting married." But it's got a lot of drinks bought for me when I'm out and about.'*

In the April issue of *Vanity Fair*, Meghan posed up with other 'Global Leaders of Tomorrow' for a cover story and was quoted saying: *'While my life shifts from refugee camps to red carpets, I choose them both because these worlds can, in fact, coexist, and for me they must.'*

In April 2017, Meghan closed down The Tig, telling her fans: *'After close to three beautiful years on this adventure with you, it's time to say goodbye to The Tig.'*

'What began as a passion project evolved into an amazing community of inspiration, support, fun and frivolity.'

'You've made my days brighter and filled this experience with so much joy.'

'Keep finding those Tig moments of discovery, keep laughing and taking risks, and keep being "the change you wish to see in the world."'

'Above all, don't ever forget your worth – as I've told you time and time again: you, my sweet friend, you are enough. Thank you for everything.'

In April 2017, Harry, William and Kate promoted their 'Heads Together' mental health charity with a series of interviews. In one, Harry revealed he was 'very close' to a breakdown as he struggled with his mother's death: *'I can safely say that losing my mum at the age of 12, and therefore shutting down all of my emotions for the last 20 years, has had quite a serious effect on not only my personal life but my work as well.'*

'I have probably been very close to a complete breakdown on numerous occasions when all sorts of grief and sort of lies and misconceptions and everything are coming to you from every angle.'

'My brother, bless him, he was huge support to me.'

'He kept saying this is not right, this is not normal, you need to talk to someone about stuff, it's OK.'

'I took up boxing, because everyone was saying boxing is good for you and it's a really good way of letting out aggression. And that really saved me because I was on the verge of punching someone.'

'My way of dealing with it was sticking my head in the sand, refusing to ever think about my mum, because why would that help?'

'I thought it's only going to make you sad, it's not going to bring her back.'

'And then I started to have a few conversations and actually, all of a sudden, all of this grief that I have never processed started to come to the forefront and I was like, there is actually a lot of stuff here that I need to deal with.'

Appearing on the front cover of *Pride* magazine's July issue, Meghan said: 'It makes me think of the countless black jokes people have shared in front of me, not realising I am mixed.'

'I feel an obligation now to talk about discrimination…or even to talk about the fact that most people can't tell that I'm half black.' Once they realise I'm mixed race they're like "Oh, sorry!"'

'Because I've just been this ethnically ambiguous fly on the wall, listening to everything that you're saying that you wouldn't have comfortably said had you known I was black, so I don't care if I'm fair-skinned and I don't care what it is, that's who I am, that's my family.'

'My hope is for the world to get to a place where it's colour blind.'

'While my mixed-race heritage may have created a grey area surrounding my self-identification, keeping me with a foot on both sides of the fence, I have come to embrace that.'

'To say who I am, to share where I'm from, to voice my pride in being a strong, confident mixed-race woman.'

'That when asked to choose my ethnicity in a questionnaire as in my seventh-grade class, or these days to check "other" I simply say, "Sorry world, this is not 'Lost' [**American television drama**] and I am not one of 'The Others.' [**from 'Lost'**] I am enough exactly as I am."'

In interviews to mark the 20th anniversary of Princess Diana's death, Harry said: *'The last thing I wanted to do was read what other people were saying about my mother.'*

'One of the hardest things for a parent to have to do is just tell your children that your other parent has died.'

'How you deal with that, I don't know.'

'But he [**Prince Charles**] *was there for us, he was the one, out of two, left.'*

'He tried to do his best and to make sure we were protected and looked after.'

In one interview, Harry said of walking behind Diana's coffin: *'No child should be asked to do that.'*

But in another programme, BBC documentary *Diana 7 Days*, he said: *'I'm very glad I was part of it.'*

'I think it was a group decision but I was proud of it.'

He recalled Diana's last phone call home to him saying: *'It was probably about tea-time, and I was a typical young kid running around playing and it was like, right ah, I really wanna play.'*

'If I'd known that was the last time I was going to speak to her, the conversation would have gone in a very different direction.'

'I have to live with that for the rest of my life.'

On Elton John's 'Candle in the Wind' during Diana's funeral: *'It was like someone firing an arrow.'*

'Elton's song was incredibly emotional and nearly brought me to the point of crying in public, which I'm glad I didn't do.'

At the end of September 2017, Harry and Meghan appeared together for the first time at a public event, the Invictus Games in Toronto, Canada, where 550 competitors from 17 countries took part in 12 sports.

Meghan beamed with pride as Harry told the audience of competitors, their friends and families: *'You are all winners and don't forget that you are proving to the world that anything is possible.'*

'Invictus is about the dedication of the men and women who served their countries, confronted hardship, and refused to be defined by their injuries.'

'It's about the families and friends who faced the shock of learning that their loved ones had been injured or fallen ill – and then rallied to support them on their journey of recovery.'

'And above all, Invictus is about the example to the world that all service men and women – injured or not – provide about the importance of service and duty.'

The Prince said his life changing moment came on a flight home from Afghanistan in 2008, after his first deployment there in the army.

He was confronted with the coffin of a dead Danish soldier,

and three British troops all in induced comas with missing limbs, wrapped in plastic. *'The way I viewed service and sacrifice changed forever,'* he said.

'I knew it was my responsibility to use the great platform that I have to help the world understand and be inspired by the spirit of those who wear the uniform.'

Speaking at an addiction and mental health centre in Toronto, he said: *'It seems we suffer from a culture where a pill will fix everything.'*

'There has to be a better way than just giving out anti-depressants.'

In a speech at the WE Day event in Toronto, Harry implored youngsters to look up from their phones and stand up for what they believe in: *'You know that differences of opinion, of circumstance, of race and religion are to be respected and celebrated.'*

'You know that in a clickbait culture, we cannot waste time sharing and drawing attention to things that make us angry, or that we know to be false.'

'You all know that it's great to "like" things on social media, but that it's more important to look up from our phones, to get out into our communities, and to take real action – to stand up for what you believe in.'

'I get that the challenges we face sometimes seem complex and even scary, especially when we don't know who to turn to for answers.'

'I know that while this generation of young people wants to make the world a better place, you often struggle to get your voices heard.'

'I know that you, more than any previous generation, care deeply about the health and sustainability of the planet you're going to inherit.'

'And I see that you're frustrated that entrenched mind-sets are not keeping pace with the urgency of the threats to our environment.'

'But today you are all saying no to pessimism and cynicism. Here in Toronto – with both WE Day and Invictus – we are saying yes to optimism, yes to hope, and yes to belief.'

'Today's generation of young people is the most connected, most energised, and most confident the planet has ever known.'

At the end of the Games, Harry vowed to continue them, saying: *"It's been on another level, amazing. The sky's the limit.'*

In October 2017, Harry visited the Danish capital of Copenhagen for two days, and warned youngsters about the perils of social media: *"It's crazy and scary.'*

'It's like a mental running machine that they can't get off.'

'You wouldn't put your body through such a workout.'

'I'm the last person to say "ban it", but people are suffering from mental fatigue and getting burnt out.'

His thoughts on Twitter: *'I try not to take any notice of Twitter but it's very difficult.'*

On a visit to the Danish Veterans Centre, Harry was reunited with competitors from the Invictus Games, including wheelchair rugby player Maurice Manuel, whose bald head the Prince kissed in Toronto.
Joking that Maurice was growing his hair to avoid being kissed again, Harry said: *'My lips have never recovered!'*

In the October 2017 issue of *Vanity Fair* magazine, Meghan gave an interview in which she admitted she was in love with Harry. She had been working on 'Suits' for seven years: *'Seven Canadian winters! A long time for someone who grew up in Southern California.'*

Talking about the pressures of being Harry's girlfriend she said: *'It has its challenges, and it comes in waves – some days it can feel more challenging than others.'*

'And right out of the gate it was surprising the way things changed.'

'But I still have this support system all around me, and, of course, my boyfriend's support.'

'My parents had been so supportive, watching me audition, trying to make ends meet, taking all the odds and ends jobs to pay my bills.'

'I was doing calligraphy, and I was a hostess at a restaurant – and all those things that actors do.'

'My father knew how hard it is for an actor to get work, so he above all people was so proud that I was able to beat the odds.'

As a child, Meghan watched her father Thomas, a lighting director, at work on a sitcom: *'Every day after school for 10 years, I was on the set of 'Married…with Children', which was a really funny and perverse place for a little girl in a Catholic school uniform to grow up.'*

'What's so incredible, you know, is that my parents split up when I was two, but I never saw them fight.'

'We would still take vacations together.'

'My dad would come on Sundays to drop me off, and we'd watch 'Jeopardy!' eating dinner on TV trays, the three of us … we were still so close knit.'

On the South-Central riots in Los Angeles in the early 1990s: *'They had let us home from school during the riots and there was ash everywhere.'*

'I said, "Oh my God, mommy, it's snowing!" and she said, "No, Flower, it's not snow – get in the house."'

On their relationship: *'I can tell you that at the end of the day I think it's really simple.'*

'We're two people who are really happy and in love.'

'We were very quietly dating for about six months before it became news, and I was working during that whole time, and the only thing that changed was people's perception.'

'Nothing about me changed. I'm still the same person that I am, and I've never defined myself by my relationship.'

'We're a couple, we're in love.'

'I'm sure there will be a time when we will have to come forward and present ourselves and have stories to tell, but I hope what people understand is that this is our time.'

'This is for us.'

'It's part of what makes it so special, that it's just ours.'
'But we're happy.'

'Personally, I love a great love story.'

'I don't read any press. I haven't even read press for 'Suits'.'

'The people who are close to me anchor me in knowing who I am. The rest is noise.'

'My parents crafted the world around me to make me feel like I wasn't different, but special.'

'At almost every photo shoot they would airbrush out my freckles. I've always loved my freckles!'

In October 2017, Harry was interviewed at the Obama Foundation in Chicago. Asked about his mother's death, and his role as a royal, he said: *'I don't think I understood it.'*

'I think what happened to my mum probably put me a step back.'

'Thinking well how could someone who did so much for the world and so much for everybody else be treated like that by a certain institution?'

'So, it takes a bit of getting used to.'

'But as I say once you understand the privileged position that you are in you then get to spend the rest of your life earning that privilege and giving back and also gaining the trust and respect of the general public and then using that position for good.'

'My understanding of service and duty became really ingrained and was given to me by my service to the military because that's what it's all about.'

Asked why he didn't head up 200 charities instead of a few under the Royal Foundation he said: *'In today's world, you have to be much more hands on.'*

'If you end up working individually for, let's say, 200 charities in today's world, that kind of dilutes the impact that you can have.'

'What our foundation is all about and what our platform is all about is encouraging people to come together, to work together, so that there's less competition within that sector whether financially or otherwise.'

'And say, Right guys, you are all doing the same thing, please let's get round a table, talk to each other, work it out and come up with a long-term strategy.'

Question: *'A Royal Foundation – another charity do we need it?'*

'*My motto is exactly that – why another charity? Our foundation is not another charity. We are not trying to take up any more space.*'

'*We agree that the charity sector is quite full at the moment!*'

'*We are trying to use our foundation as a platform to bring people together and effect change.*'

Harry on Diana: '*I think she had a lot in common with everybody but also she certainly listened.*'

'*You saw in a very, very short space of time she was like a vacuum going round, sucking up all the information, all the criticism, all the issues, all the positions and the negatives from everybody, and then putting her name and her platform towards some of the biggest issues which have never been talked about.*'

'*We do, in society, we suffer from this illusion, or reality I suppose, while some problems are so big that no one wants to get involved.*'

'*She was the one who changed that and I will always look up to her as being my ideal role model and everything that she did and the way she did it was having an impact and making a difference.*'

'*Because of the position that we are in and the role that we play as part of our institution you are in it for life.*'

'*You are not in it for four years or in it for eight years, you are in it for life and therefore you have a bigger longer platform than politicians, let's say.*'

'We can't get involved in certain things but she re-wrote the rule book and she pushed the boundaries more than ever before and boundaries need to be pushed more than ever.'

'She was successful and I think all of those people who she was working for were incredibly grateful for her pushing the boundaries.'

'It's not easy. In today's world boundaries need to be pushed more than ever before.'

On November 27 2017, The Prince of Wales announced that Harry and Meghan were engaged. Later that day, they posed up for photos in the Sunken Garden at Kensington Palace.

Asked when he knew Meghan was 'the one' Harry replied: 'When did I know she was the one? The very first time we met.'

Meghan said they were: 'So very happy,' **and Harry added:** 'Thrilled, over the moon.'

The couple then went inside from the cold, to be interviewed by the BBC's Mishal Husain. Asked about Harry's proposal, Meghan said: 'We were just roasting a chicken, just an amazing surprise, it was so sweet and natural and very romantic. He got on one knee.'

A mutual friend had introduced them in the summer of 2016. 'It was definitely a set-up, it was a blind date,' **said Meghan.**

Meghan: 'Because I'm from the States, you don't grow up with the same understanding of the royal family.'

'And so while I now understand very clearly there's a global interest there, I didn't know much about him.'

'And so the only thing I had asked was, "Well, is he nice?"'

Harry: *'I'd never watched 'Suits', I'd never heard of Meghan before. When I walked into that room and saw her, and she was sitting there, I was like, okay, I'm going to have to really up my game here!'*

Meghan: *'I think for both of us though it was really refreshing because, given that I didn't know a lot about him, everything that I've learnt about him I learnt through him as opposed having grown up around different news stories, or tabloids or whatever else.'*

'Anything I learnt about him and his family was what he would share with me and vice versa. So, for both of us it was just a really authentic and organic way to get to know each other.'

Harry: *'It was hugely refreshing to get to know someone who isn't necessarily within your circle, doesn't know much about me.'*

Meghan: *'I think that very early on when we realised we were going to commit to each other, we knew we had to invest the time and the energy and whatever it took to make that happen.'*

Meghan: *'I think I can safely say, as naïve as it sounds now, having gone through this learning curve in the past year and a half, I did not have any understanding of just what it build be like.'*

Harry: *'I tried to warn you as much as possible.'*

Meghan: *'I think there's a misconception that because I have worked in the entertainment industry that this would be something that I would be familiar with.'*

'But even though I'd been on my show for, I guess six years at that point, and working before that, I'd never been part of tabloid culture, I've never been in pop culture to that degree and lived a relatively quiet life, even though I focused so much on my job.'

Meghan: *'I made the choice not to read anything, positive or negative, it just didn't make sense. And instead we focused all our energies just on nurturing our relationship.'*

Asked about the scrutiny on her mixed-race background, Meghan said: *'Of course it's disheartening, you know it's a shame that that is the climate in this world to focus so much on that or that that would be discriminatory in that sense.'*

'But at the end of the day, I'm really just proud of who I am and where I come from and we never put any focus on that, we've just focused on who we are as a couple.'

Harry: *'The fact that I fell in love with Meghan so incredibly quickly was sort of confirmation to me that everything – all the stars were aligned – everything was just perfect.'*

'It was this beautiful woman just sort of literally tripped and fell into my life, I fell into her life.'

'The fact that I know she'll be really unbelievably good at the job part of it as well is obviously a huge relief to me, because she'll be able to deal with everything else that comes with it.'

'*We're a fantastic team, we know who we are.*'

Meghan: '*The causes that have been very important to me I can focus even more energy on, because very early out of the gate I think you realise once you have access or a voice that people are going to listen to, with that comes a lot of responsibility which I take seriously.*'

Asked about giving up her career: '*I don't see it as giving anything up, I just see it as a change.*'

"*It's a new chapter, right.*'

'*I've been working on my show for seven years…I have ticked this box and I feel really proud of the work I have done there and now it's time to, as you said, work as a team with you.*'

Harry: '*That sense of responsibility was a couple of months in when I know that I'm in love with this girl and I hope she's in love with me, but we still had to sit down on the sofa and I still had to have some pretty frank conversations with her.*'

'*To say look you know what you're letting yourself in for is – it's a big deal – and it's not easy for anybody.*'

'*But I know at the end of the day, she chooses me and I choose her and therefore whatever we have to tackle, together, or individually, will always be us together as a team.*'

Meghan: '*That's so nicely said, isn't it?*'

Asked about children Harry replied: '*Not currently, no!*'

Adding: *'No, of course, you know I think you know one step at a time and hopefully we'll start a family in the near future.'*

Meghan: *'His family has been so welcoming.'*

On the Queen, Meghan said: *'She's an incredible woman.'*

On the Queen's corgis: *'They were just laying on my feet during tea, it was very sweet.'*

Harry: *'I've spent the last 33 years being barked at! This one walks in, absolutely nothing...'*

On the Duchess of Cambridge, Meghan said: *'She's been wonderful.'*

Harry on Meghan's mother Dora Ragland: *'Her mum's amazing.'*

Harry on the ring he gave Meghan: *'The ring is – is obviously yellow gold because that's her favourite, and the main stone itself I sourced from Botswana.'*

'The little diamonds either side are from my mother's jewellery collection to make sure that she's with us on this crazy journey together.'

Meghan: *'It's beautiful, and he designed it, it's incredible.'*

Asked what his mother Diana would have thought of Meghan, Harry said: *'Oh yes, they'd be thick as thieves, without question.'*

'I think she would be over the moon, jumping up and down, you know so excited for me, but then, as I said, would probably been best friends with Meghan.'

'It's days like today when I really miss having her around and miss being able to share the happy news. But I'm sure she's...'

Meghan: 'She's with us.'

Harry: 'I'm sure she's with us yeah, you know, jumping up and down somewhere else.'"

On their first public engagement together in Nottingham, on December 1 2017, Meghan told waiting fans: 'Hi, I'm Meghan! It's a thrill to be here!'

When a young man with flaming red hair like Harry, shouted at him: 'How does it feel to be a ginger with Meghan?'

Harry replied: 'Great, isn't it? Unbelievable.'

Talking on Radio Four about their first Christmas with the Royals at Sandringham, Harry said: 'It was fantastic, she really enjoyed it.'

'I think we've got one of the biggest families that I know of, and every family is complex as well.'

'No, look, she's done an absolutely amazing job.'

'She's getting in there and it's the family I suppose she's never had.'

'Together we had an amazing time – we had great fun staying

with my brother and sister-in-law and running round with the kids.'

'Christmas was fantastic, the family loved having her.'

On a visit in January 2018, to the Reprezent FM community radio station in Brixton, South London, Meghan was asked by ten-year-old Grace White if she was looking forward to her wedding. *'Of course I am!'* she replied.

While chatting to male DJ YV Shells, an advocate for gender equality, Meghan said: *'You have to remind yourself that self-love is important.'*

Harry added: *'As males we have to do our part or it's not going to work.'*

TIMELINE OF HARRY AND MEGHAN'S ROMANCE:

June 2016: The couple are introduced in London, on a blind date by a mutual friend.

August 2016: Harry takes Meghan to Botswana for a five-day holiday where they fall in love.

30 October 2016: The London Sunday Express breaks a world exclusive that they are dating.

8 November 2016: Kensington Palace issues a strongly worded statement direct from Harry's heart condemning 'sexist and racist' coverage, but also confirms Meghan IS his girlfriend.

December 2016: Meghan stays with Harry in London and they are photographed together.

February 2017: The couple emerge from Soho House in London and are photographed walking down the street hand in hand.

April 2017: Meghan announces she is stopping her lifestyle blog The Tig.

May 2017: The pair are seen kissing at a polo event in Berkshire.

September 2017: In an interview with *Vanity Fair*, Meghan says: *'We are in love.'*

September 2017: They appear together for the first time at an official event, the Invictus Games in Toronto, Canada.

October 2017: Meghan meets the Queen for tea at Buckingham Palace.

November 2017: Prince Charles announces their engagement.

December 2017: The couple perform their first royal engagements together in Nottingham.

December 2017: Meghan spends Christmas Day with the royals at Sandringham.

19 May 2018: The couple wed at St George's Chapel, Windsor Castle.

Also available from Barzipan Publishing
www.barzipan.com

Diana: I'm Going to be Me

Phil Dampier

ISBN: 978-0-992613-39-6

Price: £8.95

88 pp Paperback

Diana: I'm Going to be Me tells the remarkable story of Princess Diana's life through her own words. It is now 20 years since this iconic figure died at the tragically young age of 36 in a Paris car crash. In this first ever comprehensive collection of Diana's most memorable quotes, veteran royal reporter Phil Dampier reveals the heart and soul of an incredible woman who is missed by millions around the world. From the Queen's love of corgis and life as a Royal to love, fashion and mental health, this book reveals Diana's multiple facets. So sit back and celebrate the amazing life of this never-to-be forgotten woman – the beautiful, beguiling, flawed but uniquely enchanting Diana.

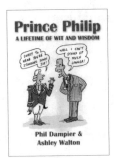

Phil Dampier &
Ashley Walton

Prince Philip: A Lifetime of Wit and Wisdom

Phil Dampier and Ashley Walton

Cartoons by Richard Jolley

ISBN: 978-0-9926133-3-4

Price: £8.95

128pp Paperback

With delicious disregard for public opinion, the Duke of Edinburgh's acerbic comments and faux pas have provided feisty fodder for cartoonists and columnists for more than six decades. Seasoned royal correspondents Phil Dampier and Ashley Walton present an affectionate portrait of an extraordinary figure who in the last century was in many ways ahead of his time, but today is seen as the last Prince of political incorrectness.

Phil Dampier &
Ashley Walton

Prince Philip: Wise Words and Golden Gaffes

Phil Dampier & Ashley Walton

Cartoons by Richard Jolley

ISBN 978-0-9573792-2-0

Price: £8.95

112 pp Paperback

His Royal Highness Prince Philip, the Duke of Edinburgh: irascible, controversial, outspoken, forthright and funny; the Gaffer, the Prince of Political Incorrectness, the Duke of Hazard, Phil the Greek. Whatever you call him – and he doesn't give a damn – you've got to love him. Now in his nineties, on he goes, undaunted, unrepentant and, if a little slower, just as amusing. This book is a celebration of the wit and wisdom of a man whose unique style, down-to-earth humour and no-nonsense approach have brought colour into our lives. This book will have you laughing out loud.